Little Pebble™

Habitats

All About
Forests

by Christina Mia Gardeski

CAPSTONE PRESS
a capstone imprint

Little Pebble is published by Capstone Press,
1710 Roe Crest Drive, North Mankato, Minnesota 56003
www.mycapstone.com

Library of Congress Cataloging-in-Publication Data
Names: Gardeski, Christina Mia, author.
Title: All about forests / by Christina Mia Gardeski.
Description: North Mankato, Minnesota : Capstone Press, [2017] | Series:
  Little pebble. Habitats | Includes bibliographical references and index.
Identifiers: LCCN 2017004645 (print) | LCCN 2017006585 (ebook) | ISBN
  9781515776383 (library binding) | ISBN 9781515776468 (pbk.) | ISBN
  9781515776772 (eBook PDF)
Subjects: LCSH: Forest ecology—Juvenile literature. | Forests and
  forestry—Juvenile literature.
Classification: LCC QH541.5.F6 G368 2017 (print) | LCC QH541.5.F6 (ebook) |
  DDC 577.3—dc23
LC record available at https://lccn.loc.gov/2017004645

Editorial Credits
Nick Healy, editor; Kayla Dohmen, designer; Wanda Winch, media researcher;
Steve Walker, production specialist

Photo Credits
Dreamstime: Bchancha, 21, Betty4240, 15, Lucidwaters, 11; Shutterstock: David Boutin, 7, Erik Mandre, 1, Ermakov Alexander, 17, Grigoriy Pil, 9, Helena-art, tree design, Henrik Larsson, 19, Jeff Feverston, cover, jurra8, 13, Sara van Netten, 5

Printed and bound in China
PO004673

Table of Contents

What Is a Forest?

A forest is a land of trees.

The trees grow close together.

Some trees have leaves.

The leaves change color in fall.

They fall off by winter.

Other trees have needles.

They stay green all year.

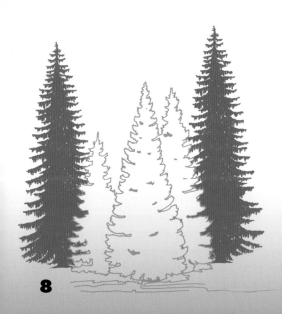

In the Treetops

The trees grow tall.

Branches cover the forest.

It is a shady habitat.

Many animals live here.

Owls spy on mice.

Squirrels pick acorns.

owl

On the Ground

Some trees fall.

Skunks live in the old logs.

Snakes hide under logs.

skunks

15

Mushrooms grow on the logs.

Deer eat the mushrooms.

Ants eat the old wood.

The wood turns into soil.

Growing Up

Animals carry seeds.

Seeds blow in the wind.

Seeds fall in the soil.

The forest grows.

21

Glossary

acorn—the seed of an oak tree

forest—land filled with trees that grow close together

habitat—the home of a plant or animal

leaf—part of a plant that grows from the stem

log—a big tree trunk that has been cut down or has fallen to the ground

mushroom—a fungus with a stem and flat cap

needle—the leaf of an evergreen tree

soil—dirt in which plants can grow

treetop—the top of a tree

Read More

Amstutz, Lisa J. *What Eats What in a Forest Food Chain*. Food Chains. North Mankato, Minn.: Picture Window Books, 2013.

Greene, Carol. *I Love Our Forests*. I Love Our Earth. Berkeley Heights, N.J.: Enslow Elementary, 2013.

Kalman, Bobbie. *Baby Animals in Northern Forests*. The Habitats of Baby Animals. New York: Crabtree Publishing Company, 2013.

Internet Sites

FactHound offers a safe, fun way to find Internet sites related to this book. All of the sites on FactHound have been researched by our staff.

Here's all you do:
Visit *www.facthound.com*
Type in this code: 9781515776383

Super-cool stuff!

Check out projects, games and lots more at
www.capstonekids.com

Index